SPOTLIGHT ON THE AMERICAN INDIANS OF CALIFORNIA

THE
CHUMASH

DOROTHY JENNINGS

PowerKiDS
press™

NEW YORK

Published in 2018 by The Rosen Publishing Group, Inc.
29 East 21st Street, New York, NY 10010

Editor: Theresa Morlock
Book Design: Michael Flynn
Interior Layout: Reann Nye

Photo Credits: Cover UniversalImagesGroup/Universal Images Group/Getty Images; p. 5 Carlos Chavez/Los Angeles Times/Getty Images; pp. 7, 17, 25 Spencer Weiner/Los Angeles Times/Getty Images; pp. 9, 14 Steve Osman/Los Angeles Times/Getty Images; pp. 10–11, 21, 23 Courtesy of the Library of Congress; p. 13 Bryan Chan/Los Angeles Times/Getty Images; p. 15 https://commons.wikimedia.org/wiki/File-Basketry_tray,_Chumash,_Santa_Barbara_Mission,_early_1800s_-_Native_American_collection_-_Peabody_Museum,_Harvard_University_-_DSC05558.JPG; p. 19 Marilyn Angel Wynn/Corbis Documentary/Getty Images; p. 22 https://commons.wikimedia.org/wiki/File:Charles_III_of_Spain_high_resolution.jpg; p. 27 https://commons.wikimedia.org/wiki/File-%22Protecting_The_Settlers%22_Illustration_by_JR_Browne_for_his_work_%22The_Indians_Of_California%22_1864.jpg; p. 29 Al Seib/Los Angeles Times/Getty Images.

Library of Congress Cataloging-in-Publication Data

Names: Jennings, Dorothy, 1961- author.
Title: The Chumash / Dorothy Jennings.
Description: New York : PowerKids Press, [2018] | Series: Spotlight on the American Indians of California | Includes index.
Identifiers: LCCN 2017019692| ISBN 9781538324547 (pbk. book) | ISBN 9781538324554 (6 pack) | ISBN 9781538324516 (library bound book)
Subjects: LCSH: Chumash Indians--Juvenile literature.
Classification: LCC E99.C815 J45 2018 | DDC 979.4004/9758--dc23
LC record available at https://lccn.loc.gov/2017019692

Manufactured in China

CPSIA Compliance Information: Batch #BW18PK For further information contact Rosen Publishing, New York, New York at 1-800-237-9932.

CONTENTS

WHO ARE THE CHUMASH?............4

CHUMASH ORIGINS 6

RELIGIOUS BELIEFS 8

TRADITIONAL SOCIETY 10

LIVING OFF THE LAND 12

MAKING TOOLS......................14

BUILDING HOMES...................18

IMPORTANT STRUCTURES 20

SPANISH ARRIVAL 22

CHUMASH MISSIONS 24

CALIFORNIA CHANGES HANDS........26

PRESERVING CULTURE 28

THE CHUMASH TODAY...............30

GLOSSARY 31

INDEX.............................32

PRIMARY SOURCE LIST...............32

WEBSITES..........................32

CHAPTER ONE

WHO ARE THE CHUMASH?

The Chumash are a group of American Indians that traditionally lived in and around the Santa Barbara Channel area in California and spoke languages from the Hokan language family. Their name comes from the name Michumash, which means "a people who make shell bead money."

Chumash society was once widespread and **diverse**, with at least eight **dialects** spoken and many variations across communities. Over the centuries, the Chumash society and **culture** were affected by the **invasion** of their lands by European and American settlers. During the 18th and 19th centuries, the Chumash suffered huge losses due to disease and war. They were forcibly relocated, enslaved, and killed. The Chumash have fought to recover from the many **injustices** they suffered in the past. Today, their culture continues to change as they work to honor their past and protect their future.

In this photo, a man in traditional dress dances at a celebration at the Chumash Interpretive Center in Thousand Oaks, California.

CHAPTER TWO

CHUMASH ORIGINS

No one knows when the first Chumash appeared. **Anthropologists** believe that people arrived in the Alaska area in North America between 40,000 and 13,000 years ago. Over many generations, they moved south, and by about 8,000 years ago, some had settled in what is now California. About 1,000 years ago, a group of the people who'd settled in California came to share very similar tools, practices, and beliefs. The Chumash **descended** from these people.

The early Chumash had a religious story that explained the origin of their people. They believed that a female god called Hutash created humans from seeds. Hutash sent some of the people she'd created across the Santa Barbara Channel by making a rainbow for them to walk on. Some people fell into the ocean, but Hutash turned them into dolphins to save them from drowning. Religious beliefs showed how the Chumash understood their place in the world.

This modern Chumash man is performing a traditional dance at a Hutash Festival in Ventura, California.

CHAPTER THREE

RELIGIOUS BELIEFS

Chumash elders taught that the universe is made of three worlds stacked on top of each other. The uppermost world is filled with powerful gods, such as Moon and Sun. The middle world consists of land and ocean. This is where the Chumash live. The lower world is filled with dark, threatening beings. The Chumash religion focused on the need to balance the power that existed in the universe. If the power went out of balance, sickness, death, and ruin would follow.

Chumash worshiped through songs and dance. Their musical instruments included flutes, rattles, and whistles. Nearly all holidays and rituals were connected to their religion. Religious holidays were filled with feasts, dances, and celebrations. Ceremonies marked the journey that people make from birth to death, as well as the changing seasons.

These Chumash men are performing the traditional Dolphin Dance.

CHAPTER FOUR

TRADITIONAL SOCIETY

People in Chumash communities were assigned to certain social groups. The smallest social groups were families, which were combined into larger groups called clans. The Chumash believed that important spiritual animals such as bears and eagles had created their clans. Each clan was assigned special jobs. The most honored clans selected one of their members to be the village leader, who was called a *wot*.

Both women and men served as *wots*. *Wots* were aided by a group of advisers called the *antap*, which was made up of respected community members such as religious leaders, doctors, and **astrologers**. The *wot's* most important helper was called the *paha*. The *wot* and *antap* served as a community's government. Sometimes, different Chumash communities formed temporary partnerships. A *wot* who controlled several villages was called a *paqwot*. Every community controlled a territory where only its members could hunt and gather.

This mural in Lompoc, California, was created to show how the Chumash people traditionally lived.

CHAPTER FIVE

LIVING OFF THE LAND

Most of the things the Chumash needed could be found near their homes. Chumash settlements were built near rivers and streams so that freshwater was easily available. They gathered native plants to eat and use. Some of the things they used were cattail pollen, walnuts, chamomile, and pine nuts. They hunted wildlife such as deer, bears, birds, mountain lions, and rabbits. Those who lived on the shoreline hunted dolphins, otters, seals, and sea lions. They also caught fish.

The Chumash prepared food in several ways. They ground many wild plants into powder or dried them in the sun to preserve them for later seasons. Stone pans, stone bowls, baskets, and hot rocks were used to cook, and animal fat was used to grease cookware. Most cooking was done with an open flame, over which items were steamed or grilled. Salting and smoking **techniques** were used to preserve fish and meat.

This Chumash storyteller is wearing a coyote skin. Coyotes are one of the many animals that are traditionally important to the Chumash people.

CHAPTER SIX

MAKING TOOLS

The animal parts the Chumash didn't eat, such as bones, were used to make tools, needles, hairpins, fishhooks, and furniture. Animal skins were used to make clothing and blankets, and bird feathers were used to make arrows, capes, and headdresses. Seashells became bowls and jewelry, and clamshells were used to make knives. Sharkskin served as sandpaper, and sinew, a kind of muscle, was stripped from animals and used to make bowstrings.

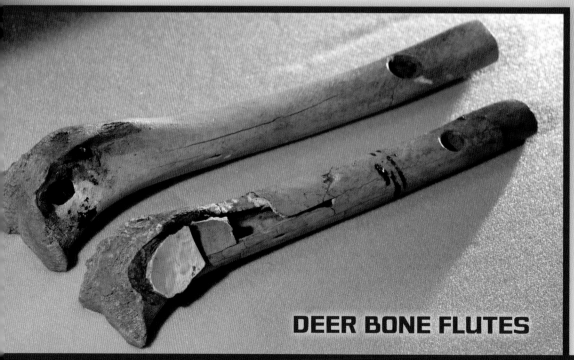

DEER BONE FLUTES

This basket was made by the Chumash sometime in the early 1800s.

The plant world provided other raw materials, such as grass, rushes, and willow shoots, which were collected and woven into baskets with detailed patterns. Wild hemp, milkweed, nettles, and yucca plants were made into strings and ropes that could be used to make nets, bags, and other woven objects. Some baskets were waterproofed by coating them with tar. Pine sap was used as glue and giant wild rye stems were made into arrows.

Stone and wood were other important resources to the Chumash. They shaped stones such as granite, sandstone, and basalt into useful objects. **Mortars** and **pestles** were made to grind nuts and seeds into flour. A rock called soapstone was used to make pipes and bowls. Soapstone was useful because it didn't crack when heated or cooled.

Wood was used to make cradleboards for babies. It was also used to make boats and oars. Plank canoes, or *tomols*, were designed to hold up to 12 adults. They were 12 to 30 feet (3.6 to 9.1 m) long. *Tomols* were made of tree trunks split into planks and trimmed using stone tools, sharp shells, and antler hammers. Sharkskin was used to finish the planks before they were glued together with tar. Red ochre plant mixed with pine sap was used to seal the outside of the *tomol*.

These young Chumash people are paddling a *tomol* off the mainland near Santa Cruz Island.

CHAPTER SEVEN

BUILDING HOMES

The Chumash used reeds and poles to build their homes. Houses were circular, and ranged from 10 to 20 feet (3 to 6.1 m) across. Inside, the walls were lined with low wooden platforms with reed mats that served as beds. A fire pit, or hearth, was dug in the middle of the room. The flames kept the house warm and provided heat for indoor cooking during bad weather. A hole in the center of the roof allowed the smoke to escape and let sunlight in. When it rained, a piece of animal skin was used to cover the opening.

Community leaders had huge houses up to 50 feet (15.2 m) across. These homes were usually surrounded by warehouses and working areas where people made tools and crafts. Large Chumash villages had many houses organized into neat rows separated by straight paths.

This Chumash hut is located at the La Purisima Mission State Historic Park, Lompoc, California.

CHAPTER EIGHT

IMPORTANT STRUCTURES

Each Chumash community had a special, sacred area called a *siliyik* that was used for ceremonies. The *siliyik* was a circular area surrounded by tall walls made from reed mats. Colorful banners fluttered from the flagpoles surrounding the *siliyik*. Religious leaders performed ceremonies inside the *siliyik*. At this time, most people sat outside.

Every village also had a sweat lodge. This was a small structure that was partially buried in the ground. To enter, one had to use a ladder. Inside, a fire produced smoke and heat. People came there to cleanse themselves spiritually and heal when they were sick. Villages also had cemeteries where graves were marked with painted poles.

The Chumash didn't build walls to defend their villages. When they were at war, the people took shelter in nearby caves. If an enemy burned down the village, its people would rebuild.

Early Chumash often painted cave walls with symbols. These pictures are called pictographs.

CHAPTER NINE

SPANISH ARRIVAL

When the Spanish reached the Chumash region in 1542, the Chumash and the Europeans developed a long and complicated relationship. For more than 200 years, between 1542 and 1769, the American Indians who lived by the Santa Barbara Channel occasionally traded with the crews of passing ships. Some interactions were friendly; others ended in violence.

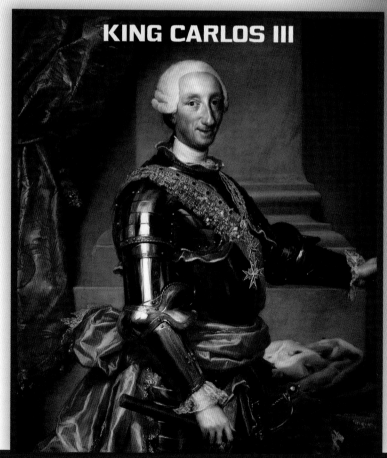

KING CARLOS III

This picture shows the Mission San Luis Obispo as it appeared in 1936.

In 1769, the Spanish, under the reign of King Carlos III, took control of California. Spain didn't have the money, soldiers, or colonists needed to **conquer** and occupy the region. Instead, the Spaniards hoped to gradually turn the American Indians into Spanish citizens by leading them to adopt their religion and culture. The first Spanish settlement among the Chumash was established at San Luis Obispo in 1773. This settlement was a religious community called a mission. Spanish missions were used to spread their religion to the American Indians and teach them to replace hunting and gathering with agriculture.

CHAPTER TEN

CHUMASH MISSIONS

Through the missions, the Chumash were introduced to many aspects of the European way of life, including European **technology**, plants, and animals. Some Chumash people were converted by the religious teachings of the Christian missionaries. Some were drawn to missions because they offered comfortable living situations. Others joined the mission communities as a way of partnering themselves with the powerful Spanish. The missions were run by the Spanish with the help of traditional Chumash leaders who took on new jobs as mayors and city council members.

Some Chumash rejected the missions, wishing to preserve their traditional way of life. By the end of 1787, however, new missions had been established at San Buenaventura, Santa Barbara, and La Purisima. The growing missions made it more difficult for the Chumash to maintain traditional ways of life. Those who rejected the missions traveled east into California's Central Valley or lived secretly in the rugged mountains.

These sculptures of a Chumash man and a Spanish Franciscan friar, or religious leader, are located at the Ventura County Museum of History and Art. The exhibit was created to teach visitors about the Spanish missions in California.

CHAPTER ELEVEN

CALIFORNIA CHANGES HANDS

In 1822, Spain gave control of California to Mexico. The Mexican soldiers and settlers treated the Chumash and other American Indian groups very badly. The Chumash were forced to work for little or no pay. The Mexican government put the army in charge of dealing with the Chumash and the missions exploded in violence. The Mexican settlers took almost everything the Chumash possessed. Soon, a war between Mexico and the United States would bring about even worse conditions.

In 1846, the U.S.- Mexican War ended in a treaty that forced Mexico to give control of California to the United States. The United States government believed that all American Indian people should be removed or killed. The discovery of gold in California in 1848 brought a wave of newcomers who drove the Chumash off their lands and killed them. The government passed laws to allow white settlers to take American Indians as slaves.

The California gold rush was a tragic event in American Indian history. This illustration made in 1864 shows American settlers killing American Indians.

CHAPTER TWELVE

PRESERVING CULTURE

In 1855, the United States government set aside a tiny piece of land for the Santa Ynez Chumash Reservation. Only 99 acres (40 ha) of land belonged to this last remaining community of Chumash, which was considered an independent nation. The people who lived there were encouraged, and sometimes forced, to adopt American culture.

The Chumash were banned from speaking their native language. Chumash children were sent to boarding schools where they were trained to abandon their traditional culture and adopt American beliefs and lifestyles. Although the pressure to reject the beliefs and history of their ancestors was great, the Chumash did not forget who they were or where they came from. The modern Chumash people have made great strides in reclaiming their cultural **heritage**.

This Chumash medicine woman is leading a sunrise blessing ceremony in Malibu, California, where a model of a traditional Chumash village was created in 2005.

CHAPTER THIRTEEN

THE CHUMASH TODAY

The Chumash saw themselves as part of the natural world, rather than its owners. They relied on the resources that the environment supplied to survive but understood that they must balance their needs with those of other living things so these resources wouldn't run out. When the European, Mexican, and American settlers invaded California, their treatment of the land and the Chumash people upset this balance and had tragic consequences. Despite their suffering, the Chumash endured.

During the last century, the Chumash have fought hard to protect their civil rights. Many have worked to protect their sacred places from development and to reclaim the bones of their ancestors and their **artifacts** from museums. They take pride in their traditions and the history of their people.

GLOSSARY

anthropologist (an-thruh-PAH-luh-jist) A scientist who studies the history and society of humans.

artifact (AR-tuh-fakt) Something made by humans in the past that still exists.

astrologer (uh-STRAH-luh-jur) Someone who believes the stars and planets have an influence on human affairs.

conquer (KAHN-kur) To take over by force.

culture (KUHL-chuhr) The beliefs and ways of life of a certain group of people.

descend (dih-SEND) To come from a certain family or group.

dialect (DY-uh-lekt) A form of language spoken in a certain area that uses some of its own words, grammar, and pronunciations.

diverse (dy-VURS) Different or varied.

heritage (HEHR-uh-tij) The cultural traditions passed from parent to child.

injustice (in-JUH-stiss) An unfair or bad act.

invasion (in-VAY-shun) The act of forcibly entering or attacking a territory.

mortar (MOR-tur) A small vessel made of something hard in which things are ground with a pestle.

pestle (PEH-suhl) A tool used to grind something in a mortar.

technique (tek-NEEK) A particular skill or ability that someone uses to perform a job.

technology (tek-NAH-luh-jee) The way that people do something using tools and the tools that they use.

INDEX

A
Alaska, 6
antap, 11

C
Carlos III, King of Spain, 23
Central Valley, 24
Chumash Interpretive
    Center, 4
clans, 10

D
dance, 4, 6, 8
Dolphin Dance, 8

G
gold rush, 26

H
Hokan language family, 4
Hutash, 6

L
La Purisima, 18, 24

language, 4, 28
Lompoc, 18

M
Malibu, 28
Mexico, 26
Michumash, 4
mission, 23, 24, 25, 26
Mission San Luis Obispo, 23
Moon, 8

N
North America, 6

P
paha, 11
paqwot, 11
pictograph, 20

S
San Buenaventura, 24
San Luis Obispo, 23
Santa Barbara, 24

Santa Barbara Channel, 4,
    6, 22
Santa Cruz Island, 16
Santa Ynez Chumash
    Reservation, 28
siliyik, 20
Spain, 23, 26
Spanish, 22, 23, 24, 25
Sun, 8

T
Thousand Oaks, 4
tomol, 16

U
U.S.-Mexican War, 26

V
Ventura, 6
Ventura County Museum of
    History and Art, 25

W
wot, 10, 11

PRIMARY SOURCE LIST

Page 15
Chumash basket from the Santa Barbara Mission. ca. early 1800s. Now kept at the Native American Collection, Peabody Museum, Harvard University, Cambridge, Massachusetts.

Page 21
Painted Rock in the Carrizo Plain National Monument. Photograph by David McNew.

Page 23
Mission San Luis Obispo de Tolosa. ca. 1936. Photograph by Historic American Buildings Survey. Now kept at the Library of Congress Prints and Photographs Division, Washington, D.C.

WEBSITES

Due to the changing nature of Internet links, PowerKids Press has developed an online list of websites related to the subject of this book. This site is updated regularly. Please use this link to access the list: www.powerkidslinks.com/saic/chum